W9-DCG-492

OFFICE OF THE
MAYOR

This book has been a joint effort by the Heritage Committee and the City of Yellowknife to depict Yellowknife over the last 50 years.

I feel that our heritage is extremely important to our culture and to all aspects of Northern living, and I appreciated all the hard work that has gone into creating this book.

I know that you will enjoy reading this book and browsing through the illustrations and pictures.

Yours truly,

(Ms.) P.A. McMahon
Mayor

Yel

llowknife

HOW A CITY GREW

by Erik Watt

Outcrop
The Northern Publishers

Copyright © Outcrop Ltd., The Northern Publishers,
February 1990. First edition, 1990.

All rights reserved. No part of the material covered by
this copyright may be reproduced in any form or by any
means without the written permission of the Publisher.

Design:
Ernest Burden, Outcrop

Photo Credits:
Front cover, *Fran Hurcomb, NWT Archives*.
Back Cover, Yellowknife by night, *Tessa Macintosh,
GNWT*. Inside Cover, The City of Yellowknife grew
around a successful mine. View of the Con Mine, 1937,
shows Mosher Island, background. *John Poirier, Nerco
Con Mine.*

ISBN 0-919315-22-4

Outcrop Ltd., The Northern Publishers Box 1350,
Yellowknife, Northwest Territories Canada, X1A 2N9
Printed and bound in Canada
by Quality Color, Edmonton

Dedication

To the people of Yellowknife,
past, present and to come.

Special thanks to:

David Lovell and the Yellowknife Heritage Committee
Richard Valpy and Lynette Harper, Prince of Wales
    Northern Heritage Centre
Gary Milligan, Government of the Northwest Territories,
    Culture and Communications
Bob O'Connor, Aero Arctic
Grant Horseman, Nerco Con Mine
Sheila Hodgkinson
Walt Humphries
and all our photographers, who took such a great
    interest in this project.

A portion of the profit from the sale of this book will
fund a heritage trust for the citizens of the City of
Yellowknife.

Acknowledgements

Yellowknife is one of those places that makes a truism of the old cliche that "Once a Yellowknifer (or Edmontonian, or Haligonian, or whatever), always a Yellowknifer." But few ex-residents of anywhere keep closer touch with friends who've remained than former Yellowknifers.

That fact came home repeatedly in the writing of this book, and nowhere so markedly as in the search for the *Lindquist* after whom Lundquist Road in Old Town is named. (The sign at the top of the street spells it *Lundquist*, but that's another story.) Most of the present-day Yellowknifers I spoke to had no idea; a few remembered he'd been a miner, but no one recalled his first name. Nor could city hall's computer.

Then someone suggested I try Carolyn England of Yellowknife Hardware. "I remember the family," she said, "but not his first name." She paused, then brightened. "But Helen Lundstrom would. She's in Edmonton now, and I just heard from her the other day. I have her number right here . . ."

Helen Lundstrom remembered the Lindquists, but not that first name. "But Mrs. Ivar Johnson would," she said, "and she's in Kelowna."

"It's John," said Mrs. Johnson, a few minutes later. "Our kids grew up together." Mission accomplished.

Yellowknife, a famous book published in 1967 by the late Ray Price, was a valuable guide in tracking down the people and the stories of YK's early days, as were the files of the Prince of Wales Northern Heritage Centre and custodian Richard Valpy. But much of this material came from Yellowknifers who are still here, years later.

Listing those people who contributed to this book without omitting someone who did would be an impossible task, but the unofficial editorial board who helped so much in the final stages, at our daily coffee sessions in the Miner's Mess of the Yellowknife Inn, deserve special mention. They include Jack Adderley, D'Arcy Arden Junior (still "Sonny" to the men who knew his long-departed father), John Brophy, C. B. "Shorty" Brown, Alderman Mike Byrne, Albert Eggenberger, Smokey Heal, Walt Humphries, Frank Lafferty, Doug Leonard, Jim McAvoy, Tom Pagonis, Mike Piro, Randy Pon, Ivan Rand, Jack Sigvaldason, Dave Smith, Jack Tees, George Tuccaro, Merlin Williams, Ron Williams and Chuck Vaydik.

Some are oldtimers (Smokey Heal marks his 50th anniversary in Yellowknife this year), some were born here and some, like me, are relative newcomers. But they, their wives and their children, and people like them, are what make Yellowknife what it is today and will be tomorrow — a city with a zest for life. No resident, no matter how temporary, will ever forget living here.

Erik Watt
Yellowknife
February 1990

When Outcrop started business in this beguiling Northern city in 1975, Mayor Fred Henne and Harvard Budgeon, manager of the Yellowknife Inn, were making the first co-ordinated attempts to record the city's history. Mabel Braathen, Barb Bromley, the Warner family, Mike Piro, Tom Doornbos and Arnold Smith all shared Fred and Harvard's enthusiasm and passed it along to two eager newcomers, who had planned to stay just a year or two...

Today, the the City boasts a Yellowknife Heritage Committee, and they are largely responsible for en-couraging us to attempt this book. The idea came from a show of photographs mounted by Gary Milligan in 1984. The show, called *Yellowknife, Then and Now,* included photos taken in the forties by Henry Busse, and dupli-cate views taken in the eighties by Milligan. A selection of these images forms the basis of this book.

Yellowknife is unique among Canada's capital cities. Its history stretches back only sixty years, and people are still alive today who remember the first days of the little mining camp on the rock. Almost everyone has a photo album and at least one or two great stories to tell, documenting the rise of the city. But each year, the list of early alumni grows shorter. Sometimes memory plays tricks, and stories recorded here may some day change.

This book, published with the co-operation and assistance of Mayor Pat McMahon and the Council of the City of Yellowknife, is a tribute to all the people, pioneers and newcomers alike, who continue to give Yellowknife its unique aura of living history — the story of Canada in the 20th century.

Ronne Heming
Marion LaVigne

February, 1990

Foreword

A city's heritage is not represented by a stale collection of musty books and old buildings. Rather, heritage is a part of our everyday life that can provide endless enjoyment. To understand heritage is to have an awareness of the relationship of the activities of the past to the activities of the present. Yellowknife's collective heritage is the result of the efforts of individuals who came for individual reasons and who, by settling here, laid the social, economic and cultural foundations for today's city. This book illustrates the links between their past and our present.

A book such as this doesn't write itself, but is the result of a great deal of individual effort. The original concept was based on a series of then and now photographs prepared by Gary Milligan in 1984. The original idea for a book was developed during conversations with Art Sorensen in 1987. Financial support was obtained from the City of Yellowknife through the efforts of Mayor Pat McMahon in 1989, and Ronne Heming provided the creative force that brought the parts together. Numerous other individuals have been active in the creation of this product, in the best tradition of community involvement.

Enjoy!

David Lovell
February, 1990

I came up here for

NWT Archives

John Poirier

a couple of weeks ...

OLDTIMERS WOULD NEVER
RECOGNIZE THE NEW "CITY WHERE
THE GOLD IS PAVED WITH STREETS."
□
TENT FRAMES AND RIVER SKIFFS
DOTTED THE SHORES OF
YELLOWKNIFE BAY IN THE EARLY
1930s.

Yellowknife!

"YK" rates that exclamation mark. This is surely the most exciting capital city in Canada, a bustling, fascinating community of close to 15,000 on the rugged north shore of Great Slave Lake.

Don't let that population figure fool you. Yellowknife *is* a city, with most of the creature comforts you'll find far to the south, smack in the middle of the awesome wilderness of the Northwest Territories. The land — which is what Northerners call everything outside the NWT's sixty scattered communities — is within walking distance from anywhere in the Territorial capital.

Don't let that lonesome dot on the map convince you this is the end of the world. Yellowknife is North, all right, but it's about seventy kilometres closer to San Francisco than it is to the North Pole. The native Dene of the region never did build iglus, and you'll have to fly another six hundred kilometres north if you hope to see a live polar bear.

Outcrop

Derek Bodington

Dene and Metis make up fifteen percent of our population. Our Dogrib name is Sòmba K'e — which means "Money Place." We're that, too, even though the name of our most famous street — Ragged Ass Road — has been a better description in the past.

Yellowknife really is the place where yesterday rubs shoulders with tomorrow, in the words of its civic slogan.

Elbow up to the bar in one of our posh dining lounges and chances are you'll squeeze in between a bearded prospector just in from the Barrens and a visiting federal cabinet minister in a business suit.

What's more, you'll probably strike up an easy conversation with either of them. Despite the formality a huge civil service population creates, Yellowknife is still a city where anyone can fit in, almost instantly.

In part, that's due to isolation. True, there's a highway to Edmonton, and more than thirty flights a week to that provincial capital — plus others to Winnipeg. But Yellowknife *is* isolated. A handful of families at Dettah, twelve kilometres away on the eastern shore of Yellowknife Bay, and the Dene community of Rae-Edzo, one hundred kilometres to the northwest, are the city's closest neighbours. And in the break-up and freeze-up seasons on the Mackenzie River, Yellowknife is accessible from the south only by air.

Fran Hurcomb

NWT. AIR GREW FROM A SINGLE OTTER BASED IN YELLOWKNIFE TO A TERRITORIAL AIRLINE UNDER FOUNDER BOB ENGLE.

□

AN AIR FORCE DAKOTA THAT CRASHED AT THE FIRST TEE SERVED AS A CLUBHOUSE FOR GOLFERS IN THE 1940s.

□

HOUSEBOATS PROVIDE ONE ANSWER TO HIGH LAND COSTS, BUT BREAK-UP AND FREEZEUP ON YELLOWKNIFE BAY PRESENT CHALLENGES TO COMMUTERS.

□

JUST ABOUT EVERYONE TRIES GARDENING.

Fran Hurcomb

Michael Sharpe

11

Fran Hurcomb

NOT LONG AGO, PROSPECTORS SAILED
INTO YELLOWKNIFE BAY ABOARD
WHATEVER WOULD FLOAT. NOW
WEEKEND SAILORS CRUISE THE EAST
ARM OF GREAT SLAVE LAKE IN SLEEK
RACERS AND GLEAMING YACHTS.

□

The Yellowknife Highway crosses the wide Mackenzie at Fort Providence, by ferry in summer and ice road in winter. It can be closed up to three months of the year, depending on whether the ferry can operate or the ice is thick enough for cars and trucks to cross.

Though it's usually their quest for an independent life that brought them North in the first place, few of YK's non-native people have extended families in the North. Yellowknifers, as a result, tend to form another kind of family, one based on just being here.

The Subarctic climate serves to accentuate this bonding process. Geographically, Yellowknife lies in semi-desert country, despite the many nearby lakes; average annual precipitation, including snow, is only twenty-six centimetres. And temperatures range to extremes. In summer they can hit plus thirty. But in winter the mercury plunges as low as minus fifty-six degrees Celsius!

Michael Sharpe

FOLK ON THE ROCKS, AT LONG LAKE,
COMBINES LONG SUMMER DAYS WITH
A FESTIVAL OF NORTHERN MUSIC.

□

IN SUMMER THE SMALLER LAKES
WARM TO SWIMMING TEMPERATURE,
AND GREAT SLAVE LAKE IS GOOD
FOR A QUICK DIP.

□

CRUISING HOME,
SHORTLY AFTER MIDNIGHT.

Fran Hurcomb

Ernest Burden

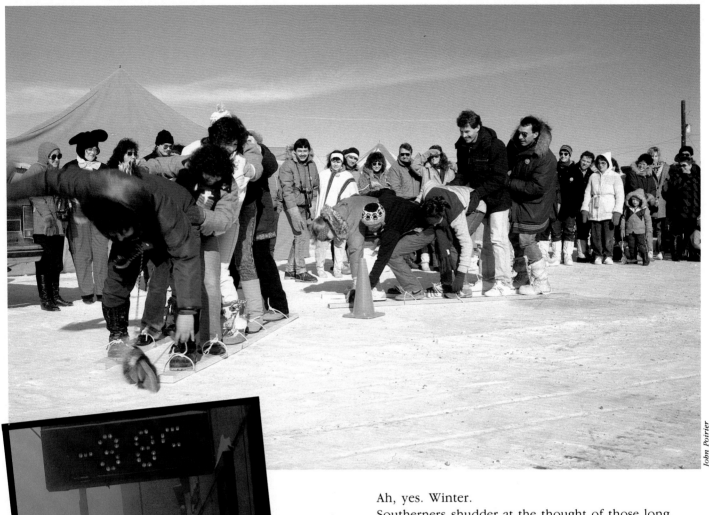

John Poirier

Michael Sharpe

CARIBOU CARNIVAL IN MARCH
SIGNALS THE END OF WINTER.

□

DRESSED FOR THE WEATHER, A
YELLOWKNIFER HEADS HOME IN THE
WINTER DUSK.

Ah, yes. Winter.

Southerners shudder at the thought of those long, dark, freezing days. So do Northerners.

But a funny thing happens each year when the mercury drops to minus forty for the first time. People adapt. They bundle up in multiple layers of Arctic clothing and go about their business.

YK's cosmopolitan population includes Vietnamese, Californians, South Americans, Australians, Pakistanis, Indians, Africans, Arabs and possibly more Newfoundlanders than St. John's. All of them discover that minus forty isn't all that bad, if you dress for it. But dressing for it is a learned skill.

You can easily pick out the newly arrived on the first days of winter. They're the people, blue with cold, hurrying about in miniskirts or southern-style topcoats.

A month later, bundled up in parkas, windpants, fur mitts and boots, they're indistinguishable from the oldtimers — and walking to work because they enjoy the fresh air.

Winters can be eight months long in bad years, and by December 21 — the shortest day of the year — it's only daylight from about 11 a.m. to 3:15 p.m. You go to work in the dark and come home in the dark. But there are seven more minutes of daylight on December 22 than there were on December 21, and every day after that gets longer.

Michael Sharpe

Fran Hurcomb

Fran Hurcomb

WHEN THE TEMPERATURE REALLY DROPS, THERE'S LIKELY TO BE ICE FOG, HERE COLOURED BY A LOW-HANGING SUN.

□

WITH THE TENTH LARGEST LAKE IN THE WORLD FOR A RINK, SKATERS CAN TAKE TO THE ICE IN EARLY NOVEMBER.

□

SKIERS SPROUT LIKE FLOWERS ON YELLOWKNIFE'S GROOMED TRAILS AS SOON AS THE SNOW FLIES.

Chris O'Brien

Fran Hurcomb

PAST MIDNIGHT AT MIDSUMMER ON
FRAME LAKE, IN THE HEART OF
YELLOWKNIFE.

□

YELLOWKNIFE'S GROWING SEASON IS
SHORT, BUT LONG SUMMER DAYS
BRING OUT THE GARDENERS.

By April there's only an hour or two of darkness left, and by June 1 you can play golf at midnight. (YK's rocky fairways and sand "greens", to say nothing of its ball-stealing ravens, offer unique challenges.) You don't see true darkness again until late July.

The rumour persists in Yellowknife that there's a musty old bylaw somewhere in the City archives that prohibits sleeping between June 21 and September 1. A glance down the main street, Franklin Avenue, at four a.m. might convince you no one does! There are plenty of cars and people abroad, in the golden light.

Half of Yellowknife's fascination is that it's the crossroads of the North. Any day of the week, summer or winter, you'll find people from all over the world on its streets, in its restaurants, shops, office buildings and high-rise apartments.

The Miner's Mess at the Yellowknife Inn is the traditional downtown meeting place for Northerners and visitors alike. The story goes that if you spend enough time there, you'll meet everyone you ever knew.

Royalty, salespeople, pensioners and billionaires find their way to this city on the ancient granite of the Precambrian Shield.

The British royal family is particularly fond of Yellowknife. The NWT capital is one of the few places on earth where the Duke and Duchess of York have felt free to go for a late-evening walk downtown with only a guide and personal bodyguard as company. The Yellowknifers they passed waved or said hello and left them alone to enjoy themselves.

But it's the old Yellowknife, still here despite the onrush of modern development, that lures visitors North. And it's the old Yellowknife spirit that makes many of those visitors decide to stay.

Ask anybody — oldtimer or five-year resident — how he or she chose Yellowknife as home and the answer is almost always, "I came up for a couple of weeks, but . . ." And they'll give you a shrug and a sheepish grin.

Fran Hurcomb

YELLOWKNIFE'S CITY HALL HAS A
VIEW OF FRAME LAKE.

□

THE POST OFFICE, AT FRANKLIN AND
49TH, IS STILL THE BEST PLACE TO
MEET JUST ABOUT ANYONE.

□

BILL CARPENTER'S KENNEL HELPED
BRING BACK THE ESKIMO DOG, NOW
A RECOGNIZED BREED IN CANADA.

Fran Hurcomb

Fran Hurcomb

First

John Poirier

people, first visitors.

IN WINTER, AS MANY AS TEN
THOUSAND CARIBOU WANDER SOUTH
FROM THE ARCTIC COAST TO THE
NORTH SHORE OF GREAT SLAVE LAKE.

☐

Yellowknife is named for a group of Dene who once hunted the surrounding lands, fishing Great Slave Lake and travelling into the Barrens with the seasons. They engaged in adventurous trading, ranging boldly north to Great Bear and beyond: their implements were made of native copper, obtained from Inuit on the Arctic Coast. Relatives of the Chipewyan, they were a people distinct from the Dogrib and Slavey Dene whose territories bordered theirs. The copper knives they made led the explorer Samuel Hearne to call these Dene "Yellow-knives." (Alexander Mackenzie saw the same implements in another light: he dubbed the Dene of the North Great Slave region "Redknives." Somehow a city dubbed "Redknife" just wouldn't seem like home!)

In fact, it was these copper knives that brought Hearne across the Barrens from Hudson Bay on an epic journey in the years 1770 to 1772. He'd first seen them in the hands of Chipewyan trappers who brought furs to him at Fort Prince of Wales. When the people told him there were copper deposits near the Arctic Coast, Hearne set out to find them. In the company of the Chipewyan chief, Matonabbee, he followed the chains of lakes east of Great Slave to Contwoyto and at last to the Coppermine River.

Samuel Hearne failed in his effort to locate the fabulous ''mine.'' His return to Prince of Wales took him to the shores of Great Slave, within marching distance of the gold that lay so near the surface in Yellowknife Bay. But a weary Hearne trekked off across the ice of the East Arm, and Yellowknife's secrets remained so for a century and a half longer.

It's almost certain that a fur trader named Peter Pond was the first non-native to set foot on the sector of the ancient Canadian Shield that is now Yellowknife. Here, the bones of the Earth show through: the world's oldest rocks, 3.962 billion years old, lie just three hundred kilometres north.

Pond, journeying north from Fort Chipewyan on Lake Athabasca, explored and mapped Yellowknife Bay in 1785. The following year he built a cabin on the north shore of Great Slave Lake just east of Wool Bay which lies some thirty kilometres southeast of the present-day city. Like Fort Resolution, at the delta of the Slave River on the big lake's south shore, Pond's cabin served as an outpost camp for the North West Company's post at Fort Chip. Today it is known as Old Fort Providence.

Pond's outpost had been abandoned for some months when Alexander Mackenzie set out from Chipewyan in the spring of 1789 to find Dehcho, the great river that today bears his name. He was accompanied as far as Providence by another Nor'Wester, Laurent Le Roux, with a canoe full of trade goods.

Le Roux was left to re-open the post while Mackenzie pushed on, following the river's shore all the way to the Delta, where it empties into the Arctic Ocean. The Pacific, not the Arctic, had been his goal, and Mackenzie called Dehcho ''River of Disappointment.''

The question of who named Old Fort Providence is as much a mystery as is the identity of the occupant of the lone grave on the old site: the name on its marker was long ago obliterated by the harsh gales of winter. This grave, and the faint indications of the four log buildings that once stood there, plus a few artifacts in the Prince of Wales Northern Heritage Centre in Yellowknife, are all that is left today.

The name ''Providence'' is less of a mystery. Then as now, the fishing was excellent and caribou and moose were plentiful. The sketchy records kept by the Nor'Westers indicate that Providence supplied meat and fish for other posts.

Old Fort Providence had a population of from ten to twenty men, women and children in its heyday, according to the Heritage Centre. By 1820, when it was visited by the explorer Sir John Franklin, it was already in decline — and under the flag of the Hudson's Bay Com-

GREAT SLAVE LAKE'S MOODS HELP DICTATE THE WEATHER ON ITS SHORES.

□

John Poirier

John Poirier

21

John Poirier

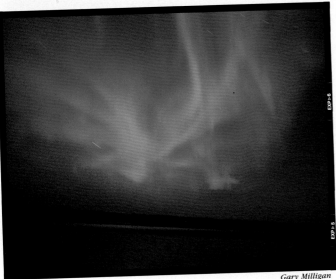

Gary Milligan

THE CAMERON RIVER AND HALF A
DOZEN OTHERS ARE STILL CANOE
ROUTES TO THE BARRENLANDS.

□

THE AURORA BOREALIS ATTRACTS
VISITORS TO YELLOWKNIFE IN
WINTER.

pany following the merger in 1805 of the Bay and the North West Company.

Frederick Wentzel, then the Bay man in charge at Providence, recruited the Yellowknife chief Akaitcho and some of his men to act as guides for Franklin's party. Franklin was bound for the Arctic coast by way of the Yellowknife and Coppermine Rivers. He and his party arrived at Fort Providence in late July and met Akaitcho on August 1 at the mouth of the Yellowknife River.

Two years later, Franklin and his emaciated survivors stumbled into Fort Providence on their return journey. Had it not been for Akaitcho and his hunters, all would certainly have starved on that nightmare trek.

The Bay's establishment at Providence consisted by then of only two clerks. It was closed down permanently the next year.

The Yellowknives suffered a terrible decline over the next century. They had long quarrelled with the Dogrib Dene of Great Slave's north shore, whom they often raided. (There was a Dogrib camp of six families or so on the present site of Dettah in Franklin's time.)

In about 1830 the less warlike Dogribs turned on their neighbours. The deadliest encounter was on an island still known as Ile des Morts, near the south shore of Great Slave's East Arm. There, under cover of darkness, the Dogribs fell on a large camp of their enemies, killing them before the half-awake Yellowknives could rally.

The Yellowknives never recovered from that blow. By the 1920s only a handful remained alive. The last camp was wiped out by an epidemic of influenza, brought in 1928 by the southern traders and prospectors who came into the area.

ASPEN, JACK PINE, SPRUCE AND
COLOURFUL LICHENS COLONIZE OUR
PRECAMBRIAN ROCK, SWEPT CLEAN
BY GLACIERS.
□
PTARMIGAN, RAVENS AND MANY
OTHER BIRDS WINTER IN THE
YELLOWKNIFE AREA.

John Poirier

Fran Hurcomb

John Poirier

Fran Hurcomb

... And there it was!

CON MINE CELEBRATED FIFTY YEARS
OF OPERATION IN 1986.

□

GIANT YELLOWKNIFE MINES POURED
ITS TEN THOUSANDTH GOLD BRICK
IN 1986.

The Trail of '98, later mining rushes at Great Bear Lake and Goldfields, Saskatchewan, the conscientious work of three Dominion geologists, and a storm on Yellowknife Bay — all played a part in the founding of "the city where the gold is paved with streets."

It was the Yukon gold rush that brought a prospector named B. A. Blakeney to the Yellowknife River in 1898. He stayed long enough to collect samples from an outcropping about fifteen kilometres upriver and sent them back to the Geological Survey of Canada in Ottawa for examination.

One of those samples was assayed at 2.158 Troy ounces of gold per tonne (half an ounce per tonne is well worth mining today.) But Blakeney headed for the Klondike by the gruelling back-door route — down the Mackenzie and over the mountains into the Yukon — and he never returned.

Michael Sharpe

In 1905, J. Macintosh Bell of the Geological Survey arrived to make the first mineral survey of Great Slave Lake's north shore. He found evidence of gold, enough to send two prospectors named Gibbons and Thomas back into Yellowknife Bay for another look in 1915. They discovered one narrow, gold-bearing quartz vein, but it was so small they didn't bother to stake the property.

Aircraft began to open up the North in the 1920s. By 1928, Consolidated Mining and Smelting Company Limited — today's Cominco — had two crews of prospectors at work on Walsh Lake, just north of the present city. An occasional independent prospector was camping on the peninsula or on Latham Island, which had become a convenient spot at which to cache supplies for parties working inland.

Then, in the fall of 1929, Gilbert LaBine followed up another Macintosh Bell report and discovered a body of pitchblende on the east shore of Great Bear Lake. That discovery would break the Belgian world monopoly on radium, a precious element found in the pitchblende. LaBine and a prospector named C. H. St. Paul staked their claims the following spring, and the Great Bear mining rush was on.

More than three hundred men, most of them desperately broke and willing to gamble everything to escape the Great Depression, descended on Great Bear in the next two years. A few stayed on, to work at LaBine's Eldorado Mine or the El Bonanza silver mine. But by 1933 the majority headed south again, by boat, barge or plane if they could afford it. Many could not, but arranged to work their passages. A few travelled south on foot, living off the land.

Among these were C. J. Baker and Herb Dixon. These two heard there was prospecting around Yellowknife Bay and headed in that direction, hoping to find work or a ride Outside.

Flying over the route they took today, you can try to imagine what they went through on that month-long trek. Their only food was what they could shoot or catch. They covered five hundred kilometres of muskeg, forest and rocky terrain, with myriad lakes and rivers to be skirted or forded. There were few trails and even fewer people and a bad fall could mean disaster. But the flies would not have been bad, since they travelled in early fall. They pushed on, taking samples every time they encountered an interesting formation and checking them each night after they'd set up camp.

Derek Bodington

PROSPECTORS LOOKING FOR GOLD
WORKED IN PAIRS, EQUIPPED WITH A
TENT, CANOE, RIFLE AND FISHING
TACKLE.
(ABOVE)

□

RAT LAKE, NAMED FOR ITS PLENTIFUL
MUSKRATS, NEAR CON MINE, 1988.
(LEFT)

Then came the night they camped on the shore of Quyta Lake, some fifty kilometres north of the Yellowknife River's mouth.

Fifty-one years later, Baker described that evening in a letter to the *Toronto Star*.

Baker had taken some samples that day from a promising quartz outcrop. After supper, he put the chunks of quartz into a gold pan, placed it on the campfire and roasted the samples to make them easier to work with. Then he and Dixon broke the rock into fragments and pulverized the fragments with a mortar and pestle. They added water and began to swish the mixture back and forth in the pan so that its heavier elements would sink to the bottom.

"And there it was," Baker recalled. "The little speck of Yellowknife gold that started it all!"

At Yellowknife Bay, they met a mining promoter named Bernhard Day and a crew of prospectors he'd hired that summer. Day had been running a motorized barge into the bay to supply Consolidated's crews. The rumours he'd picked up had persuaded him to get into the prospecting business himself.

When he saw Baker and Dixon's samples Day lost no time in hiring them. He sent the two prospectors back to stake the area around their find. Then, their work done, the pair took their money and headed Outside.

C. J. Baker was back the following spring to work for Major Lockie Burwash, manager of Yellowknife Gold Mines, the new subsidiary of Bernhard Day's transportation company.

In late September of 1934, Baker and a prospector named Hugh Muir set out by canoe and ran into a fierce storm that forced them to seek refuge on the east shore of Yellowknife Bay, directly across from Latham Island. Still stormbound the next morning, they decided to check out some unstaked land nearby.

On a hilltop overlooking the bay, they found an exposed vein of quartz seventy-two metres long that contained visible gold.

That same month, several government parties under Dr. A. W. Jolliffe were completing survey work in the Yellowknife Bay area. Most of Dr. Jolliffe's crew were University of Manitoba students spending their first summer in the field, so he split his party into three groups. He led one and his two experienced geologists, Norman Jennejohn and Neil Campbell, took charge of the others.

Jennejohn was camped on the island in Yellowknife Bay that now bears Dr. Jolliffe's name when three prospectors, Vic Stevens, Don McLaren and Ed McLellan, spotted his tent and dropped in for a cup of coffee. When they learned Jennejohn was heading out the next day to do a final traverse of the land on the west side of the bay, they asked if they could come along. Jennejohn had no objections; he was surveying, not staking claims.

Years later, Dr. Jolliffe told the story of that final

JOLLIFFE ISLAND SERVED AS A CAMPGROUND FOR PROSPECTORS IN THE 1930s. HENRY BUSSE'S CAMERA RECORDED FUEL STORAGE TANKS AND BUSY DOCKS IN THE 1940s. BY THE 1980S, JOLLIFFE WAS HOME TO A HANDFUL OF RESIDENTS, AND HIGHWAY AND AIR FREIGHT HAD LARGELY REPLACED THE OLD BARGE TRAFFIC.

□

Fran Hurcomb

Henry Busse, NWT Archives

Gary Milligan

Nerco Con Mine

Bill Braden

CON MINE WAS ERECTED IN RECORD
TIME, AND FRED WALTON POURED ITS
FIRST BRICK IN AUGUST, 1938.

□

TODAY, THE CITY HAS SPREAD TO THE
VERY EDGE OF CON'S PROPERTY.

traverse to Yellowknife geologist John Brophy.

Norman Jennejohn's party, accompanied by the three prospectors, was working just north of Jackfish Lake — where Yellowknife's auxiliary diesel power generating station now stands — when Jennejohn spotted gold in an exposed vein. He took samples and showed them to the three prospectors — who promptly started staking claims. By the time the three were finished, they'd staked nearly sixty, 460 metres to a side.

"Don't tell anyone else," one of them urged Jennejohn, and Jennejohn agreed. Normal procedure was to publish all findings of Geological Survey of Canada expeditions the following year. There didn't seem to be anything wrong with keeping the prospectors' secret until the information became public in the usual way. He and his party packed up and made their way south to Fort Smith, to meet Jolliffe and Campbell and compare notes on their season's work.

Dr. Jolliffe was disturbed when he learned the three prospectors had asked Jennejohn to keep quiet. Keeping secret a government discovery wasn't fair, he decided.

There were quite a few prospectors in Fort Smith, preparing to head south for the winter. Dr. Jolliffe called a hasty public meeting and told them of Jennejohn's find.

Among those present was Bill Jewitt, a mining engineer for Consolidated. Jewitt couldn't go to Yellowknife himself; he was busy closing down a company camp near Fort Resolution. But he got word to G. H. "Mike" Finland, a company pilot, to meet him in Resolution.

Ronnie Heming

Nerco Con Mine

NEGUS BUNKHOUSE IN 1975, BEFORE
IT WAS RENOVATED AND PUT TO
OTHER USES.

□

CON MINE BUNKHOUSES, WITH THE
WATER TOWER IN THE BACKGROUND.

"Get over to Yellowknife Bay right away," he told Finland. "Get some stakers to work."

Finland and his mechanic flew to Yellowknife the next morning. They staked several claims before Finland flew on to Walsh Lake, picked up three Consolidated prospectors and hauled them back to Yellowknife. There was already snow on the ground, but Finland, his mechanic and the prospectors — Dave McCrea, Jack Russell and Russell's son, George — staked fourteen claims in the snow. They could only hope there was something of value underneath.

Today those fourteen claims are part of the Con Mine, which marked its 50th anniversary in 1986.

Norman Jennejohn's find, combined with Baker and Muir's discovery, catapulted a quiet bay on the north shore of Great Slave Lake into the 20th Century.

There were four footnotes to the exciting developments of September, 1934:

— Baker and Muir's find on the east side of Yellowknife Bay became Yellowknife's first mine, known as the Burwash. It helped build a city, but produced only eighty-seven ounces of gold, and shut down for good in 1937.

— A prospector named Murdoch Mosher was one of the first independents to reach Yellowknife after Dr. Jolliffe's announcement. With a helper, he staked a group of claims adjacent to the Consolidated claims. These later became known as the Rycon claims, eventually sold to Consolidated for $500,000 and a forty percent interest in the property. But Murdoch Mosher never made a cent from what turned out to be Con's most valuable property. He hired two prospectors to assess the property for him and, on their advice, let the leases lapse.

— Consolidated pulled its prospectors out of the Walsh Lake area to stake the Con minesite, and in the haste and confusion of getting the mine going, the company apparently forgot about its Walsh Lake claims. But a generation later, Yellowknife prospector Walt Humphries waited patiently until the claims expired in the 1980s and re-staked them. One showing where Con had worked yielded a sample assayed at one Troy ounce of gold per tonne in 1989.

— Consolidated at one point held the rights to today's Giant Yellowknife Mines property, which took shape around the spot where Norman Jennejohn made his discovery. The ore body at Giant is folded. The early geologists suspected this, so test drilling was done at an angle, to intersect the folds. But mining oldtimers say Con drilled the wrong way — paralleling rather than intersecting the folds. When it failed to hit paydirt, Consolidated let its lease lapse, and missed a bonanza.

Giant Yellowknife Mines poured its 10,000th gold brick in 1986. Giant is one of only a few gold mines in the world ever to reach that level of production.

We didn't

Retta (McDevitt) Ball

John Poirier

have any hours . . .

OLD TOWN FROM THE SKI HILL, 1939 AND 1989. IN THE OLDER VIEW, THE LARGEST BUILDING WAS THE THEATRE, WITH THE BAKERY DOWN THE HILL TO THE RIGHT.

☐

There was feverish activity on Yellowknife Bay in the spring of 1935.

Latham Island and the rocky peninsula were already crowded with tents, pitched anywhere there was soil to anchor guy ropes. Years later, this state of affairs would pose a nightmare when the city tried to sort those early squatters' holdings into proper lots. Even today there are few standard-sized, or even rectangular, lots in Willow Flats, the oldest part of Old Town.

Lockie Burwash's crew was busy hand-steeling at the minesite on the east side of the bay, across from Latham Island. They were planning a shaft and drift to see what lay below the gold-bearing surface vein C. J. Baker (by then better known as Yellowknife Johnnie) had discovered.

Consolidated's geologists were working on the bay's west side, trying to determine the value of the fourteen claims pilot Mike Finland and his hastily assembled crew had staked through the snow the previous fall. For many

Smokey Heal

Smokey Heal

kilometres inland and along the Big Lake's north shore, the ring of steel on rock was making life miserable for the ptarmigan, marten, foxes, wolves, bear, moose, caribou and beaver whose home this once-quiet wilderness was.

People were finding gold. Fantastic samples had come out of the long trench on the Burwash property. And hardly a day passed without rumours of gold, discovered here or there. And once the ice went out of Great Slave Lake in July, the trickle of newcomers arriving by bush plane or dogsled over the frozen lake became a torrent. Prospectors barged, boated or rafted down the Athabasca and Slave Rivers from Alberta, or drifted in from Great Bear Lake and Goldfields.

The first barges in 1935 brought much-needed heavy equipment. To that point, most exploration work had been done by hand-steeling — a slow, difficult, and dangerous technique.

The real pros, men like Claude Watt and Louis Garskie, carried their big sledgehammers in caribou-hide sheaths, and polished their handles to velvet smoothness with fine sandpaper before they started work. No one else ever touched those hammers. The hexagonal-shaped ''steels'' they used, about two centimetres in diameter and anywhere from 16 centimetres to two metres long, had chisel bits lovingly honed to razor sharpness.

Smokey Heal

COLIN BURTON AND SMOKEY HEAL
WITH AN EARLY PORTABLE DRILL, A
45 KILOGRAM WARSAW "PLUGGER"
AND ITS 90 KILOGRAM COMPRESSOR.
IT WAS CARRIED BY TWO MEN USING
A POLE, VISIBLE UNDER THE
COMPRESSOR.
(TOP LEFT)

☐

OLE HESTMO, "SINGLE-JACKING." THE
FIRST FOURTEEN METRES OF THE
RUTH MINE SHAFT WERE HAND
STEELED.
(LEFT)

☐

CLIFF BROCK, STANDING, CENTRE,
AND GORDON MCLEOD, RIGHT,
STAKED THE GIANT YELLOWKNIFE
CLAIMS AFTER COMINCO LET ITS
LEASES LAPSE. THE PHOTO WAS TAKEN
IN A TRENCH ON GIANT PROPERTY,
WITH "STEVE", COLIN BURTON AND
SMOKEY HEAL, 1940.
(ABOVE)

Louis Garskie was the entire staff of Garskie Gold Mines, an operation near the East Arm of Great Slave Lake. He crushed his hand-steeled ore between two flat-surfaced granite boulders, panning the gold out of the residue, and he kept his gold in old beer bottles so he could show it to friends.

"He wasn't cheap," says Chuck Vaydik, who knew Garskie well. "He'd always buy a round for the bar when he came out of the bush in the fall. But he didn't like to *sell* his gold; he just liked to *look* at it."

Hand-steeling could be done by one, two or three men. If a man was working alone — "single-jacking" — he sat with the steel in one hand and a short, heavy hammer in the other. Double or triple-jacking, the men changed position every eight or ten minutes, the "holder" becoming a "swinger."

Swingers stood at right angles to the holder, bringing their hammers down with full force on the end of the steel. With each hammer blow, the holder rotated the steel an eighth to a quarter-turn, depending on the hardness of the rock. Double-jacking, two men could drive a hole two metres deep in an eight-hour shift, then "pop" it with a stick of dynamite to enlarge the excavation.

Water was used to lubricate the steel. The word "Mud!" was the signal for the men to change positions and scoop the pulverized rock out of the hole with a long, spoon-shaped instrument, before resuming work.

A piece of burlap with a hole in it covered the hole and prevented rock chips and water from squirting up into the holder's face. But "dog-ears," fragments of metal that curled away from the end of the steel as the hammers battered it, were a constant threat. If they weren't cleared away regularly they could be as deadly to the seated holder as bits of shrapnel.

In triple-jacking, the swingers had to be absolutely precise, landing their blows on the steel in perfect coordination. A miss could cost the holder two or three fingers — or worse. And distractions like swarming mosquitoes simply had to be ignored; neither the swingers nor holder dared to allow anything to take their minds off their tasks.

Normally, hand-steeling was done to a depth of about sixty centimetres, just enough to expose a section of unweathered rock for examination. But K. L. "Smokey" Heal remembers hand-steeling on the Ruth Mine, some seventy kilometres east of Yellowknife. "We dug the first fourteen metres of the shaft by hand-steeling," he says.

The Ruth Mine's narrow shaft, sunk at an angle fifteen degrees off the vertical, was just big enough for two men to work at a time. "We had no power," Heal recalls. "So we used spruce poles for rails and hand-winched the bucket up our pole track to the top to dump the muck (excavated rock.)"

By 1936, the Burwash crew had sunk a thirty-six metre deep shaft with a thirty metre drift running north from its bottom. But the eighty-seven ounces of gold they recovered from the surface trench was all the gold they ever found. The mine was finally abandoned in 1937.

By then, the Con Mine across the bay was well underground and work had started on its mill, thanks to a gutsy mine manager named W. M. Archibald.

The year before, poring over the geologists' reports, mining engineer Bill McDonald had told Archibald he thought Consolidated had the makings of a mine. Archibald, staking his future on his decision, ordered the supplies and equipment for a mill to be shipped North before Con had even sunk an exploratory shaft. It was a gamble unprecedented in Canadian mining history.

That gamble paid off handsomely on September 5, 1938, when Con poured the first gold brick ever produced in the Northwest Territories.

When the smaller Negus Mine came into production in 1939, Yellowknifers thought they had it made. Permanent buildings had begun to spring up on Latham Island and in Peace River and Willow Flats (the former named because most of its inhabitants came from the Peace River country of northern Alberta, the latter for its trees.)

Yellowknife had become an incorporated village, with a five-man council, in 1938. Its first school board was elected the same year and promptly hired a teacher named Mildred Hall to take over the one-room log school.

Gordie Latham's Corona Inn had plenty of competition by then; rooming houses and restaurants were proliferating. They included the Busy Bee Cafe, Ruth's Roving Hornet Cafe, the Squeeze Inn, Ann and Irene's, and Lil Bretzlaff's Lakeview Cafe. Vic Ingraham, who'd lost

OLD TOWN'S ROCK, FROM BACK BAY: 1940s, 1984, 1990.

□

TOP, VIC INGRAHAM'S YELLOWKNIFE HOTEL DOMINATED THE SCENE, LEFT. NOTE SUTHERLAND'S DRUGS, THE WHITE BUILDING IN CENTRE FOREGROUND, WHICH IS NOW THE WOODSTOVE SHOP IN WILLOW FLATS. THE LARGE WHITE BUILDING ON THE RIGHT WAS THE MOVIE HOUSE.

□

CENTRE, 1984. INGRAHAM'S HOTEL BAR WAS OPEN TWENTY-FOUR HOURS A DAY IN THE EARLY 1940s. THE BUILDING WAS REPLACED AFTER A FIRE IN 1949, BUT IT BURNED DOWN AGAIN NEW YEAR'S DAY, 1969. A MONUMENT TO NORTHERN PILOTS NOW STANDS WHERE THE WATER TOWER WAS.

□

TODAY, THE ROCK IS HOME TO THOSE WHO LIKE THE VIEW. THE SMALL BUILDINGS JUST RIGHT OF CENTRE WERE ONCE ACTUALLY INSIDE THE OLD THEATRE.

Fran Hurcomb

Henry Busse, NWT Archives

Gary Milligan

Gary Milligan

The Kettlewells

Mabel Braathen

BANKERS HAD NO HOURS IN 1946.

□

VIC INGRAHAM, WITH RIVAL
RESTAURANTEURS ANN AND IRENE.

both legs and several fingers when his schooner blew up on Great Bear Lake in 1934, was establishing himself as Yellowknife's leading hotelman.

There were lumber companies, a drugstore, general stores, laundries. The Cinnamon brothers had a brisk haulage business, and were cutting hay on Cinnamon Island to feed their horses. There was even a branch of the Bank of Toronto — a square log building still standing on Otto Drive today and, like the rest of Yellowknife then, operating largely by its own rules.

Allen Lambert, retired chief executive officer of the Toronto-Dominion Bank, was one of the YK bank's early managers, and he has fond memories of the institution.

"We didn't have any hours," he recalls. "The clerk and I lived in a tiny room at the back of the building, and if someone wanted to make a deposit or withdrawal, he'd just come over and knock on the door.

"It might be two in the afternoon or four a.m.; it didn't matter. If it was the middle of the night, one of us would get up and serve him."

Reita (McDevitt) Ball

Michael Sharpe

JACK SIBBETT'S YELLOWKNIFE
BAKERY, 1939. IT WAS ONE OF DOZENS
OF BUSINESSES WHICH SPRANG UP TO
SERVE THE LITTLE MINING CAMP.

□

THE GREAT SLAVE CRUISING CLUB
ACQUIRED THE *SILVERBELLE,* AND
MOUNTED HER ON A BARGE, IN 1988.
PART OF THE NORTH'S MARITIME
HISTORY, SHE SAILED GREAT BEAR
LAKE AND GREAT SLAVE LAKE FOR
OVER 40 YEARS.

And then, in September, 1939, the Second World War broke out. The miners were suddenly in uniform. The fuel and supplies the mines needed were largely diverted to the war effort. By 1942, the Negus Mine was the only YK mine still in production. Shuttered buildings and failing businesses were threatening to make Yellowknife a ghost town.

But Yellowknifers weren't quitters. They hung in — and they were still here when the war ended in 1945.

Off came the shutters. In poured new people and returning veterans. The Con Mine reopened and the community, which had seemed close to oblivion, was suddenly back in business.

Sanitation had grown into a real problem, even before the war, in Old Town. Raw sewage, running down over the rock, had thoroughly polluted Yellowknife Bay. In 1939, YK's first doctor, Ollie Stanton, demanded that the new council pass a sewage control bylaw. But the rock that underlay most of Old Town meant prohibitively expensive blasting had to be done if sewer and water systems were to be installed. Nobody did it. (Surface water lines are used today in summer.)

Old Towners, by and large, preferred booze to water, anyway. But Magistrate Fred Fraser (after whom Fraser Tower, YK's first highrise, is named) knew Yellowknife couldn't get by for long on trucked water, even in 1939.

Up the hill from where the town had sprung up, there was sandy soil in which sewer and water lines could be economically installed. So Fred Fraser began what was almost a one-man campaign for a new townsite. He finally persuaded the reluctant Territorial Council (then Ottawa-based and little more than a branch of the federal Department of Northern Affairs and Natural Resources) to do a survey.

The survey of the site (known as Fraser's Folly and identified for years after as "Blunderville" on city maps) was completed in 1945. Vic Ingraham, whose Old Stope Hotel below the present-day Pilots' Monument was doing a roaring trade, started work on a new hotel in "New Town" (the Ingraham Hotel is today the core unit of the modern Yellowknife Inn). And a newcomer opened New Town's first business, in 1946.

His name was Jacob "Jack" Glick, and his pioneer establishment was the Veterans' Cafe — made out of two former U.S. Army prefab Dallas huts (relics of the Canol pipeline), sheathed in plywood and eaveless, which he skidded up the hill from Old Town.

Jack Glick didn't know it then, but he had just inaugurated a trend. Many a Yellowknife building sits today on its second — or third, or fourth — site, its original clapboard, log or shingled walls concealed beneath new siding. It used to be cheaper to hire a 'Cat and move, rather than build.

Glick built the Gold Range Hotel atop his root cellar, which still serves as the hotel's basement. He constructed a new ground floor, but the hotel's upper floors

ELIOTT-HAYES HARDWARE LOADS
FREIGHT FOR A MINING CAMP,
ABOARD ASSOCIATED AIRWAYS'
BELLANCA SKYROCKET, LATE 1940s.

□

WOOD FOR MINE TIMBERS, BOILERS
AND DOMESTIC HEAT WAS SCARCE.
CREWS CUT AND HAULED BY 'CAT
TRAIN ROUND THE CLOCK, SLEEPING
BY TURNS IN THE TAR-PAPERED
CABOOSE.

on one side are higher than those on the other —
because they were formerly two Negus Mine bunkhouses
of different ceiling heights. The restaurant started out as
an Old Town rooming house.

Mining fever ran high in those early postwar years.
Giant Yellowknife Mines was sinking its first shaft, across
Back Bay from Peace River Flats, and would begin production in 1948. A favourite pastime among prospectors
was timing the bush planes that roared in and out of the
bay, their passengers close-mouthed claim-stakers who
often wouldn't even tell the pilots where they were
headed until they were airborne. Knowing the speed of
any given aircraft and noting the direction in which it
disappeared, the watchers could closely estimate where a
plane had been when it returned. Armed with this information, they might well charter planes themselves, to
check out the areas in question. You never knew when
one of the secretive stakers had found something
interesting.

Yellowknife kept on growing. Just about anything that
would fly or float or cross the ice in winter brought the
newcomers in.

Mike Piro made one of the more bizarre treks North.

Piro had served overseas with the Royal Canadian Air
Force. He'd just returned from the Yukon, where he'd
worked as a mechanic, when a passing vehicle caught
his eye on Edmonton's Jasper Avenue in the late summer
of 1947. It was a tracked Alligator, an amphibious
vehicle developed during the war by the U.S. Army for
landing supplies and heavy equipment on enemy
beaches. Painted on its side was the name of its new
owner, Yellowknife Jewel Prospecting Syndicate.

Piro, intrigued, tracked down the Alligator's owner,
mining promoter Edward Albert Hartley. "What's
with the Alligator?" Piro asked.

Hartley was happy to explain. He had two Alligators,
he said, plus two smaller amphibious Ducks (U.S. infan-
try landing craft), four surplus Bren gun carriers
(Canadian-built light armoured patrol vehicles) and pon-

John Poirier

Courtesy Mike Piro

JACK GLICK'S GOLD RANGE HOTEL
IN 1987.
(TOP)

□

MANY A FORTUNE WAS MADE ON
LAND IN YELLOWKNIFE. NEW TOWN
LOT PRICES HAVE RISEN FROM $65 TO
$65,000 IN FORTY YEARS.

toons and deck sections for bridging streams. He was heading for some promising gold claims he had north of Fort Rae. And, yes, he *could* use a good mechanic.

Which is how, a few days later, Piro found himself rattling north to Waterways, Alberta, four hundred and fifty kilometres north of Edmonton aboard the Northern Alberta Railways' infamous train. (Passengers swore the engineer and fireman ran a trapline and stopped at every culvert to check their traps. Piro's ride took thirty-six hours, and served to strengthen the legend.)

"We hired a river pilot at Waterways," Piro recalled, "and launched our flotilla, loading our Bren carriers onto rafts made from bridging equipment, which the Alligators pushed downstream.

"That pilot certainly knew the rivers. I'm sure we ran into every sandbar between Waterways and Great Slave Lake!"

The fleet drove ashore at Fort Fitzgerald, Alberta, to cross the twenty-four kilometre portage to Bell Rock, just north of Fort Smith. Then they churned on to Fort Resolution, at the mouth of the Slave, where the Alligators and their cargo were loaded aboard barges for Yellowknife. The Ducks, Hartley said, would cross Great Slave under their own steam.

Mike Piro got to ride in one of the Ducks.

It was calm when they set out, but a wind was coming up. The residents of Fort Resolution had warned them about the savage gales that batter the lake in fall.

About four hours out of Resolution, after Piro observed that they'd passed the same island at least twice, their pilot conceded he was lost. He didn't possess a map of Great Slave, it turned out.

They'd already discovered that the Ducks, with precious little freeboard, weren't designed for crossing sixty-five kilometres of open water. Furthermore, Hartley had apparently not thought to include lifejackets amid all his gear.

A bush plane buzzed overhead, flying north. "Must be heading for Yellowknife," the pilot assured his queasy crew. They followed the plane until it vanished.

The day wore on and the wind stiffened. They were riding metre-and-a-half waves now, and shipping a bit of water. Their bilge pumps and the Ducks' propellers were working all right, but they were a long way from the islands that dot the entrance to the lake's East Arm. They were acutely aware that their armour-plated Ducks would sink like stones if the pumps quit. Then, what they'd taken for a small island on the horizon ahead grew into a motorized scow, towing a barge towards Yellowknife.

Darkness fell not long after, and the wind kept up. The crew desperately navigated by the bobbing stern light of the scow, praying the pumps would keep working. Finally there were more lights ahead — Yellowknife! They'd made it.

Almost twenty-four hours after leaving Fort Resolution, the two Ducks rose from the water in front of the Lakeview Cafe in Old Town at four a.m. They trundled ashore, headlights blazing. A couple of slack-jawed drunks were watching.

"I bet they both swore off, right then," Piro grins.

Piro swore off Duck travel then and there, too. The next spring, when Hartley set off across the ice to the North Arm and headed north over frozen lakes and rivers to his claims, Mike Piro was working for Frame and Perkins, YK's first garage. He'd developed a real liking for solid ground.

Hartley almost made it. Everything but one Bren carrier got as far as Slemon Lake, just seventy-five kilometres south of his property. But break-up overtook them and Hartley's rusting flotilla is still hopelessly mired in muskeg.

Smokey Heal, a Yellowknifer since 1940, also knew about Great Slave. He used to work on the 'Cat trains that hauled YK's winter freight from Hay River before the Yellowknife Highway was opened in 1960.

The slow-moving tractors and the sleds they pulled could take a month for that treacherous crossing, depending on the state of the ice and the weather. Most of the ice was solid enough, but pressure ridges — up to six metres high — and potentially deadly cracks criss-crossed its surface.

"When we ran into a pressure ridge we'd have to follow it until we found a low spot," Smokey said. "Then we'd level off the ridge, get some planks across and drive one of the 'Cats over, to winch the sleighs to the other side."

He didn't bother mentioning what it was like to be

Fran Hurcomb

EXP-5

EXP-6

Smokey Heal

Mike Piro

Derek Bodington

John Poirier

FROM TOP LEFT, CLOCKWISE:
TOURING YELLOWKNIFE BY BOAT,
1989; CON MINE SENT ITS GOLD BARS
TO THE YELLOWKNIFE POST OFFICE
BY DOG TEAM IN THE 1940s; THE
CANADIAN CHAMPIONSHIP DOG
DERBY AT CARIBOU CARNIVAL, 1980s;
CURRY CONSTRUCTION BOMBARDIER
JUMPS A CRACK IN THE ICE ON THE
RUN TO HAY RIVER WITH ADOLPH
DUESTERHUS AT THE CONTROLS, 1955;
HARTLEY'S ALLIGATORS SETTING OUT
FOR SLEMON LAKE, SPRING, 1948.

□

working with an axe or shovel in the midst of a gale on the unprotected ice. Or in temperatures that could plummet to minus sixty. But he had vivid memories of the *latest* ice-crossing he ever made — in May, 1947.

"We had a hard winter that year, and break-up was late," Heal remembers. "The first barges wouldn't be in until July (in good years, the main body of ice on Great Slave doesn't usually break up before mid-June), and we thought we could squeeze in one more trip near the end of April.

"We got away from Hay River all right. Each of the two 'Cats was towing seven or eight sleds — more than usual, but the runners slide a lot easier when the weather warms up in spring. There were seven of us, four 'Catskinners, two swampers — me and another guy — and a cook.

"We made pretty good time at first because the pressure ridges form in the same places year after year, and we knew where we had to travel. But then the weather turned really warm, and pretty soon we were splashing through overflow. And it didn't help much when the Mounties flew out from Yellowknife, landed beside us and told us we'd have to turn back. The ice was going in Yellowknife Bay.

"It helped even less when we learned there was open water at Hay River, and all along the south shore!"

They had only two choices: abandon the train and let the cargo and equipment plunge to the bottom when the offshore ice melted, or keep going and hope for luck, or a miracle, or maybe both. And since faint-hearted people don't run 'Cat trains across lakes that are almost inland seas, they pushed on, trying to ignore the ominous booms of the fast-weakening ice.

"We got into Yellowknife Bay on May 9," Smokey Heal recalls. "The ice was in pretty rotten shape. We had to travel all the way up Back Bay to Giant Mines before we found a bit of shore ice solid enough to risk. But we made it!"

Yellowknife N.W.T.

NWT Archives

Gary Milligan

No street for Vicky.

FRAME LAKE SOUTH SUBDIVISION, FOREGROUND. THE NEW STANTON HOSPITAL, A RED BRICK BUILDING, SITS ON FRAME LAKE.

□

YELLOWKNIFE, 1950s. THE LARGER BUILDINGS ARE: LEFT, STANTON YELLOWKNIFE HOSPITAL; CENTRE, THE EARLY YELLOWKNIFE INN; RIGHT, THE CAPITAL THEATRE (PART OF WHICH HAS NOW BEEN MOVED TO OLD TOWN); AND FOREGROUND, THE GERRY MURPHY ARENA.

Much of Yellowknife's story is told in the names of its streets and landmarks.

All YK's streets once had names: King, Queen and Bay (now Macdonald Drive) graced Old Town. But the names fell out of favour — perhaps because of the Yellowknife habit of describing location as "Bill Smith's house, next to Shirley Jones."

Streets and avenues in the heart of the New Town (the name by which Yellowknife-up-the-hill is still sometimes known today) are called by numbers instead of names. Efforts of some early councillors to model Yellowknife's street system on Edmonton's, with numbered streets running east and west and numbered avenues running north and south, eventually replaced some of the more colourful historical names applied in New Town.

But to this day, many a Yellowknifer has a hard time picturing the official centre of the city, which is where 50th Street and 50th Avenue meet. *("Oh! You must mean Franklin and Sutherland's. Or is it Franklin and the Laing Building. . .?")*

Derek Bodington

Ronne Heming

The efficiency experts got as far as 41st Street, just south of the intersection of Franklin and School Draw Avenue, and as far south as 57th Street, opposite the Aven Senior Centre, and managed to number the avenues from 54th Avenue, just east of the Fraser Tower, to 49th Avenue, which runs in front of City Hall. Then, by popular demand, they went back to names.

The early explorers are here. Although Samuel Hearne rates a street (Hearne Road on Latham Island) Peter Pond does not. Sir John Franklin claims both YK's main street and the city's largest school, Sir John Franklin High School. (Akaitcho Hall, a residence for out-of-town students, is named for Franklin's guide.)

There's a Matonabbee Street, named for the Yellowknife chief who took Hearne to the Arctic Ocean and, in Yellowknife Bay near Dettah, a Mackenzie Island (though it's better known as Ace Island, possibly as a result of some forgotten poker game).

Vicky Lepine, prospector, who in 1937 chugged into Yellowknife Bay from Great Bear Lake in a motor-powered scow, set up a laundry and became YK's first female resident, is ignored among our street names.

Marion LaVigne

TOP LEFT, OLD TOWN FROM LATHAM
ISLAND. CENTRE, ASSOCIATED
AIRWAYS' BASE WAS BUILT IN 1946 FOR
CANADIAN AIRWAYS. IT STILL STANDS
ACROSS FROM THE ONE TIME
HUDSON'S BAY STORE, NOW A
WAREHOUSE. ASSOCIATED
EVENTUALLY BECAME PACIFIC
WESTERN, TODAY'S CANADIAN
AIRLINES INTERNATIONAL. NORSEMAN
LINE THE DOCK.

□

LOWER LEFT, A SIMILAR VIEW IN 1988.
STAIRWAY TO PILOT'S MONUMENT
GLINTS GOLD IN A WINTER SUN.

□

ABOVE, RAGGED ASS ROAD, 1975.
THOUGH NAMED FOR A MINING
SYNDICATE, IT APPEARED TO DENOTE
THE STATE OF REPAIR OF SOME
HOUSING IN WILLOW FLATS.

(That may well be because she married Mounted
Policeman, Casey McKale, only a few months later.
McKale was fined sixty dollars and fired for breaching
the Mounties' tough marriage regulations for young officers.) But the second woman to live here, Joan Banke,
then the wife of prospector Red Vachon (she married
Joe Banke, a Giant Mines carpenter, after Vachon's death
in 1945) is remembered by Banke Court. She was hired
by W. R. "Wop" May to cook for Canadian Airways
pilots.

Ragged Ass Road, the city's best-known street, is
named after a pioneer mining syndicate in which
Yellowknifer Claude Watt was a partner. Neither Claude
nor his daughters, Bertha and Thelma, who rowed the
first water taxi to and from Latham Island, actually made
the streets list. But Thelma's there through her husband,
early Giant miner Jack Tees (Tees Court).

Morrison Drive, Latham Island's main thoroughfare,
honours an unlucky prospector named Frank Morrison.
In 1936, he restaked the rich Rycon gold claims, which
the equally luckless Murdoch Mosher had allowed to
lapse. But Morrison made a crucial error: he forgot that
the original owner had thirty days to restake his claims
after they expired. Morrison did his staking the day
Mosher's claims expired, and his new claims were
disallowed. (Mosher Island, near the old Negus Mine
dock, is a reminder of Mosher's mistake.)

Henry Busse, NWT Archives

Lessard Drive recalls early trapper Louis Lessard, who also ran the Rex Cafe in Old Town. Boulton Road, the extension of Morrison Drive into Rainbow Valley, is named after pioneer Giant miner Jerry Boulton.

Ingraham Drive bisects the rocky Old Town hill, atop which sits the Pilots' Monument, and passes just behind the site of Vic Ingraham's famous Old Stope Hotel. Only a rusting boiler remains of that rip-roaring bar which, in Yellowknife's boisterous heyday, never closed except between midnight Saturdays and midnight Sundays.

The early prospectors are well represented in our street names.

MacDonald Drive, the Old Town continuation of Franklin, honors Ken "Curly" MacDonald, driller and pioneer contractor, and his wife, Esther. And there are (Sam) Otto Drive, (Chuck) Vaydik Court, (D'Arcy Senior) Arden Drive, (Smokey) Heal Court, Lanky (Myres) Court, (Jake) Woolgar Avenue, (Archie) Mandeville Drive, (Danny) Bagon Drive, (Ed) Hordal Road, (Frank) Avery Court, (Emile) Dagenais Drive, (Alex) Mitchell Drive, (Jim) Bryson Road, (Cliff) Brock Drive, and (Tom Senior) Forrest Drive (the Tommy Forrest Ball Park is named after his sportsman son).

Many of those early prospectors were men who possessed other talents, as well. Danny Bagon had been a middleweight boxer. D'Arcy Arden Senior was a trapper, trader, buffalo ranger and mink rancher. Chuck Vaydik and Alex Mitchell were also artists of some repute.

VIEWS FROM THE PILOT'S MONUMENT, LOOKING TOWARD WILLOW FLATS AND UPTOWN. AT LEAST NINE BUILDINGS IN BUSSE'S 1950S VIEW STILL STOOD IN 1983. THE WHITE HOUSE, CENTRE LEFT, BEHIND THE TENT FRAME, WAS ONCE THE CINNAMON HOUSE. IN THE COLOUR VIEW TAKEN IN 1975, WEAVER'S "NEW" STORE APPEARS ON THE RIGHT.

□

Gary Milligan

Marion LaVigne

Michael Sharpe

John Poirier

The aircraft that helped put Yellowknife on the map are remembered in street names, too — Fairchild Crescent, Bellanca Avenue, Norseman Drive, Stinson Road, Anson Drive, Albatross Court, Dakota Court and Catalina Drive. The men who flew them have not done as well. Only three Yellowknife pilots make the list: bush pilots Jim McAvoy, Ernie Boffa and Max Ward, the latter an RCAF veteran who parlayed a Single Otter into Wardair Limited, at its peak Canada's third-largest national airline and top international charter carrier.

One non-Yellowknife pilot is honoured, as well.

In November, 1971, pilot Manley Showalter of Yellowknife ran out of gas near Tuktoyaktuk and made a forced landing on a frozen lake. He was unhurt and his plane undamaged, but by the time he'd contacted Tuk by radio, the armed forces had already begun a search for him. Captain S. Gitzel and a Search and Rescue Dakota with five others aboard reached Tuk just after Showalter called in.

He had plenty of food and survival gear, Showalter reported; all he needed was a drum of fuel. That could wait until the weather in the area had cleared.

But Search and Rescue had just been roundly criticized in the media for its alleged failure to press another search. Gitzel and his crew, still smarting from that criticism of their unit, were in no mood to wait.

John Poirier

NOW PART OF THE FAMILY, AIR
TINDI'S EARLY SINGLE OTTER TOOK
TRISH WARNER TO AKLAVIK FROM
EDMONTON TO BE MARRIED. CESSNA
185 STOL IN THE BACKGROUND
(TOP LEFT)

☐

DE HAVILLAND TWIN OTTERS AND
TURBO BEAVER LINED UP AT
PTARMIGAN AIR'S FLOAT BASE IN
OLD TOWN.
(LEFT)

☐

LATHAM ISLAND AIRWAYS' BEAVER.

☐

LATHAM ISLAND AIRWAYS' BEAVER
LAID UP FOR WINTER.

Sheila Hodgkinson

Derek Bodington

WILLOW FLATS LOOKING TOWARD
SCHOOL DRAW, 1940s.

□

They had little trouble locating Showalter, and began a long circle to turn into the wind and land beside him. Then, while Showalter watched in helpless horror, the Dakota flew into a fog-shrouded hill and exploded.

A civilian aircraft brought Showalter his fuel the next day, when the weather cleared. He helped load the six bodies from the Dakota aboard the rescue aircraft, refueled his own plane and flew it back to Tuk. He didn't touch the controls again for eleven years.

Gitzel Street honours this pilot who tried and failed. A stone cairn and plaque on Dakota Court, which runs off Gitzel, pays tribute to Gitzel, his crew and the other Search and Rescue crews who have risked their own lives on Northern errands of mercy.

The miners, the mining promoters, the men who hauled the supplies and the men who built the mines, as well as the early mines of the Yellowknife area themselves — the Burwash, Rycon, Con, Negus and Ptarmigan Mines — are remembered on the city's street signs, too (not Giant, though: it was a Johnny-come-lately in 1948).

Michael Sharpe

IN THE SAME VIEW IN 1989, CON'S
ROBERTSON SHAFT HEADFRAME AT
LEFT, AND FRASER TOWER AND JOHN
ANDERSON THOMSON TOWER ON THE
RIGHT DOMINATE THE SKYLINE.

□

ON A MOONLIT NIGHT IN WINTER
IT'S BRIGHT ENOUGH TO SEE
CLEARLY.

John Poirier

Michael Sharpe

Sheila Hodgkinson

Byrne Road honours Norman Byrne Senior, a legendary mining promoter who left his footprints on minesites all over the North. Lamoureux Road revives memories of tough Emile "Frenchy" Lamoureux, whose Frenchy's Transport 'Cat trains fought blizzards and cold to haul YK's freight across frozen Great Slave.

Joe Herriman, after whom Herriman Road was named, marked his 50th year as a prospector and miner in 1988; in his seventies, he was still working at Giant Yellowknife Mines. Balsillie Court, named after early Giant carpenter John Balsillie, honours a well-known Yellowknife family. Butler Road remembers longtime Cominco employee Ted Butler and his wife, Kay; (George) Taylor Road recalls another oldtimer at Giant, and Knutsen Avenue is named for pioneer mining man George Knutsen and his blacksmith brother, Andy.

Lundquist Road remembers John and Helen *Lindquist* and their daughter, Margaret Karen, who was the first child born to transplanted southern Canadians in Yellowknife. John Lindquist worked at the old Discovery Mine north of Yellowknife, as well as in YK

Many a man who came to Yellowknife to work in the mines stayed to go into business on his own. Bill Frame (Frame Lake) and Jack Perkins (Perkins Court) started Yellowknife's first garage, Frame and Perkins. Fred Henne (Fred Henne Campground) came North and worked as a mine union organizer before buying Frame

Ronne Heming

Ronne Heming

Ronne Heming

AT LEAST ONE ROLLICKING CHRISTMAS PARTY RAISED THE RAFTERS AT WEAVER AND DEVORE'S FIRST STORE IN OLD TOWN. THE OLD GAS PUMP THAT STOOD BESIDE IT IS NOW HOUSED AT THE PRINCE OF WALES NORTHERN HERITAGE CENTRE.

□

MANY STREETS IN YELLOWKNIFE ARE NAMED FOR EARLY RESIDENTS.

□

ALL THAT REMAINED OF VIC INGRAHAM'S HOTEL AFTER THE FIRE WAS THIS BOILER, NOW LOCATED BESIDE THE WILDCAT CAFE.

Pilkington, NWT Archives

Ronne Heming

EXP-10

EXP-9

THE WILDCAT CAFE (BUILT IN 1937) AS
IT WAS IN 1941. HENRY BUSSE IS
THOUGHT TO HAVE WORKED ABOVE
THE REXALL DRUGS, LEFT.
(TOP)
□
IN 1975, THE WILDCAT HAD BEEN
ABANDONED FOR MANY YEARS.

and Perkins. He wound up as mayor of Yellowknife for several terms between 1956 and 1979.

Walter and Carolyn England (England Court) opened Yellowknife's first hardware store. Ivar and Alice Johnson (Johnson Court) were in the transportation business before they started Johnson's Lumber which — like the Englands' Yellowknife Hardware — is still in business. Dusseault Court honours three Yellowknife brothers who pioneered in the taxi business — Henry "Red" Dusseault, Eddie and Al. (Al was skip of many a Territorial curling team in national championships, and chief of the volunteer fire department during the 1950s and 1960s.)

Weaver Road, named for the late Bruce Weaver, passes between Harry Weaver and Ellis Devore's original log cabin general store and the present Weaver and Devore general store in Old Town, another family-run business. Doornbos Lane is a memorial to Tjaart "Tom" Doornbos, who made his fortune hauling water in Old Town in two tin pails at twenty-five cents per bucket.

At the foot of Doornbos Lane (Tom lived for a time in the old Bay bunkhouse at the top) stands the Wildcat Cafe, faithfully restored and as busy in the summers now as it was when Willie Wylie (Wylie Road) and Shorty Stout (Stout Road) first opened its doors in 1937.

THE WILDCAT TODAY. A VOLUNTEER GROUP, THE OLD STOPE ASSOCIATION, RENOVATED THE LOG AND SAPLING BUILDING AND OPENED IT IN 1979 AS A POPULAR SUMMER RESTAURANT.

□

TOM DOORNBOS SOLD WATER TO YELLOWKNIFE RESIDENTS, AT TWENTY FIVE CENTS A PAIL, IN THE FORTIES.

□

INTERIOR OF THE WILDCAT TODAY. PILOTS, MINERS AND VISITORS STILL GATHER HERE FOR BREAKFAST, LUNCH AND DINNER.

57

NWT Archives

Derek Bodington

Like the Busy Bee and the Rex Cafe, the Lakeview Cafe is only a memory today, but Bretzlaff Lane recalls Lil Bretzlaff, who ran the Lakeview in Old Town.

Sam Bigelow (Bigelow Crescent) was an early Yellowknife barber. He once owned the properties where the Laing Building and the Gallery Building now sit, but sold them before the Government came North and property values soared. Glick Court is named after Jack Glick, who built the Gold Range Hotel.

Curry Drive recalls Del and Rose Curry, who established one of the city's oldest contracting firms, Curry Construction, in partnership with Smokey Heal.

Angus Sutherland, who'd been at Great Bear Lake during the rush of the early 1930s, opened YK's first drugstore, Sutherland's Drugs, in 1938, but never stayed to run it. The late Doug Finlayson (Finlayson Drive) acquired the business and the name in the 1940s and his family still operates it downtown.

Bromley Drive and Calder Court recall merchant Graham "Peter" Bromley, an active Boy Scout and Cub worker, and dentist Ian Calder, who drowned when their canoe overturned during a holiday trip on the Back River. Barb Bromley is still a leading Yellowknife citizen. Glowach Court honours Alex Glowach, for years a popular maintenance man in YK's schools.

Two members of the Loutitt family, the late Alex

Henry Busse, NWT Archives

LATHAM ISLAND IN THE EARLY
FORTIES. VISITORS TO THE ISLAND
TRAVELLED BY WATER TAXI.
(TOP LEFT)

□

RACINE ROAD, YELLOWKNIFE'S MAIN
STREET, 1940s, FROM LATHAM ISLAND.
(LEFT)

□

LOOKING NORTH TOWARD GIANT
MINES ACROSS BACK BAY. LATHAM
ISLAND'S CAUSEWAY WAS IN PLACE IN
THE 1950s.
(ABOVE)

□

TODAY, YOU CAN SEE THE
YELLOWKNIFE TRADING POST AND
NEW HOUSING ATOP THE ROCK ON
LATHAM.
(RIGHT)

Gary Milligan

Loutitt (Loutitt Street) and his daughter, Mabel Braathen (Braathen Avenue) are recognized for their contribution to the community. Alex carried the mail by dogteam down the Athabasca and Slave Rivers from Fort McMurray, Alberta, to Fort Smith, Fort Resolution and Hay River before moving to Yellowknife during the first gold rush; his family was one of the first in the area.

Mabel Braathen was a charter member of the Daughters of the Midnight Sun, a group of pioneer Yellowknife women famed for their annual dinner and skits, at which the mighty were quickly felled in song and dance. Their less rollicking work as volunteers at the Stanton Yellowknife Hospital was equally effective. Mabel was also an active Anglican Church worker.

Bea Daniels (Daniels Court) helped form the Metis Association of the NWT and has worked with that organization for years. She has a great sense of humour, too; YK oldtimers still chuckle about her appearance in an Ethnic Day pageant, when one half of her was dressed as a Scottish piper and the other half as a Dene woman!

Bob Borden (Borden Drive) started out as a mine accountant and bookkeeper, and wound up as a travel agent. Glen and Ted Cinnamon and Glen's wife, Mickey, have both a court and Cinnamon Island, just upstream from the Yellowknife River bridge, named after them.

A. E. "Ted" Williams (Williams Avenue) became the city's first lawyer in 1937 and, by all accounts, was one of the livelier citizens. Ray Price, in his book *Yellowknife*, notes that Williams and a prospector friend disposed of thirteen bottles of brandy in one long session in Vic Ingraham's hotel.

Ted Horton, who bought *News of the North* (today's *News/North*, one of three Yellowknife newspapers) from its founder Duke DeCoursey and also served as Mayor, made the sign list (Horton Crescent). So did John Murray (Jock) McMeekan (McMeekan Causeway). The late John Anderson-Thomson, a Dominion land surveyor who surveyed the Yellowknife Highway route and laid out much of early Yellowknife, is remembered by Anderson-Thomson Boulevard. Hamilton Drive is named for Red Hamilton, a Great Slave bargeman who first saw Yellowknife in 1933 when there wasn't a single tent in sight. He moved here in 1936 and ran a water taxi to Negus and Con Mines before there was a road to connect them to town.

Phinnie Court recalls Magistrate Laurie Phinnie of Yellowknife who was the Western Arctic's flying court until the appointment of Mr. Justice John Howard Sissons as the NWT's first Supreme Court judge in 1955. Judge Sissons and Magistrate Phinney inaugurated regular flying circuits to the settlements in 1956, a system still followed today. (Sissons Court and J. H. Sissons Elementary School commemorate the Judge; whether naming Phinnie's and Sissons' streets as "Courts" was someone's sly pun, the record does not say.)

PEACE RIVER FLATS IN THE EARLY 1950s. OLD TOWN GREW BEFORE IT COULD BE SURVEYED, AND TO THIS DAY LOT SIZES VARY. TENTS CAN BE SEEN ON JOLLIFFE ISLAND, TOP LEFT, AND THE BURWASH MINESITE IS VISIBLE ON THE FAR SHORE.

□

IN THE SAME VIEW TODAY, HOUSEBOATS ARE MOORED OFF JOLLIFFE ISLAND.

□

BELOW, COMMERCIAL FISHING CONTINUES IN WINTER, WITHIN SIGHT OF THE CITY.

Fran Hurcomb

Henry Busse, NWT Archives

Gary Milligan

Denison Court honours former Yellowknife RCMP officer John Denison, who went into trucking and then earned an international reputation as a builder of winter ice roads.

Lundstrom Court, named for Bert and Helen Lundstrom, recognizes an early contractor who built the Yellowknife Post Office and the Pilots' Monument. The oldest surviving building in the Yellowknife area was built by Bert Lundstrom and Tony Aaria in 1931, at the air radio transmitter near the Dettah Road on the Ingraham Trail. In 1944, the cabin was reconstructed on Back Bay near the Anderson-Thomson residence.

Magrum Crescent honors George Magrum, a pioneer trapper, prospector and jack-of-all trades.

Yellowknife's first teacher, Mildred Hall, opened that original, one-room log schoolhouse in 1938. The building now sits on the grounds of Mildred Hall Elementary. The late Norman J. McPherson, a popular civil servant, has an elementary school named after him, too. The Ruth Inch Memorial Swimming Pool honours a lady who contributed much to that sport in Yellowknife. Mining engineer and naturalist William McDonald, known as "old Bill Mac" in later years, has a junior high school to recall his contribution to the City.

There's an old log cabin down on Bretzlaff Drive in Old Town that's the only evidence of some of Yellowknife's earliest businesswomen — the prostitutes who followed the miners North as inevitably as the bootleggers and cardsharks did.

The cabin's a relic of a place called Glamour Alley. It was never a street as such, just a winding trail running toward Yellowknife Bay, along which were pitched four tentframes — standard canvas tents with wooden floors and sidewalls — and a small log cabin owned by a chap named Doc Griffin, and later by a lady of ill-repute called Blondie. Glamour Alley provided most of the entertainment for the miners who walked into "town" from the Negus and Con Mines on Saturday nights, stopping at Doc Griffin's illegal watering hole before carrying on down Glamour Alley.

There was an oddly easy relationship between the girls of Glamour Alley and the handful of wives and single women in legitimate jobs who constituted early Yellowknife's female population. They were women together on a raw frontier, and whenever there was a dance or major social occasion, the mine manager's wife and the ladies of Glamour Alley mixed quite freely.

In 1938, a man named Stewart demanded the RCMP close down Glamour Alley. Prior to that, there'd actually been an effort to have the district legalized!

For years, City Hall didn't know what to do about a short street in Old Town that was called Lois Lane at one end and Penny Lane at the other. Both Lois Little and Penny Aumond had lived on the street for years, and both names were accepted.

BY THE LATE 1950s, WOOD FRAME HOUSING HAD LARGELY REPLACED THE LOG CABINS OF PEACE RIVER FLATS.

□

IN 1989, A SLOUGH HAD BECOME THE FRITZ THIEL PARK, AND THE SURROUNDING AREA WAS NAMED JOSEPHINE WALCER PARK. BOTH PEOPLE WERE LONG-TIME RESIDENTS.

□

BERT LUNDSTROM AND TONY AARIA HAND CRAFTED THE OLDEST SURVIVING BUILDING IN YELLOWKNIFE, IN 1931. IT WAS MOVED TO BACK BAY FROM THE DETTAH ROAD IN 1944.

□

FRITZ THIEL PARK.
(BELOW)

Ronne Heming

Henry Busse, NWT Archives

Gary Milligan

Ronne Heming

Fran Hurcomb

Marion LaVigne

But the matter was settled in 1984, when the city marked its Fiftieth Anniversary with Homecoming celebrations that attracted former Yellowknifers from all over. One visitor was Hollywood actress Margot Kidder, who was born here. Margot was "hot." She'd just hit the bigtime in the movies, playing Superman's girlfriend Lois Lane. Council seized the opportunity and Lois Lane was made the official name.

Margot's dad, longtime mining man Ken Kidder was largely responsible for getting Yellowknife its first telephone system, just after the Second World War. But nobody named a street after him.

No one's named a street after Einar Broughton, either. His Woodyard in Old Town was one of YK's first commercial establishments. But it's doubtful that Einar, who loved his overproof rum, ever worried about that. He has the most distinctive tombstone in Yellowknife's Lakeview Cemetery.

The verse on it reads:

> He drank Old Sam
> and didn't give
> a damn.

John Poirier

THIS HOUSE IS LOCATED IN WHAT
WAS EINAR BROUGHTON'S
WOODYARD.
(TOP LEFT)

□

TODAY WOODY'S BARBER SHOP IN
WILLOW FLATS IS A WORKSHOP.
(LEFT)

□

WILLOW FLATS RESIDENTS WERE
AMONG THE FIRST IN YELLOWKNIFE
TO SPECIALIZE IN SUPER-INSULATED,
ENERGY-EFFICIENT HOUSING.
(ABOVE)

□

SLIM CAMPBELL'S HOUSE IN
WILLOW FLATS.

HISTORIC SITE
This was the home of Slim Campbell.
Slim came north in 1928 to trap and
prospect in the barrens out of Rocher
River. After being crippled by his wolf
-dog team, he supported himself by

Fran Hurcomb

John Poirier

The

Michael Sharpe

Huskies still howl.

It isn't often that a hockey player, a pair of cooks, and two waiters can change the skyline of the city they've made their home. But Shorty Brown, Newton Wong, Jimmy and Randy Pon and Calvin Mark are Yellowknifers, and in Yellowknife even the wildest dreams can come true.

C. B. "Shorty" Brown came North in 1950, to play hockey for the Yellowknife Chiefs. The Giant and Con Mines had teams, and the Chiefs were the town's team.

Neither mine was above hiring a good hockey player to beef up its team; Yellowknife, then as now, was a keen hockey town. But while the mines could put their players on the payroll (there were nearly always vacant jobs to be filled, because turnover was high), the town had to find Shorty Brown a job with mining promoter Norman Byrne. His $300 a month as a hockey player was a pretty skinny living allowance by itself.

Brown, a five-foot-zip forward, had already made a bit of a name for himself in junior hockey in the south. He

A VIEW OF TODAY'S YELLOWKNIFE
FROM FRAME LAKE.

□

SLED DOGS ARE OFTEN FAMILY PETS.

PEACE RIVER FLATS AND THE
YELLOWKNIFE SKYLINE IN THE 1950S.
THE FUTURE YELLOWKNIFE INN IS
VISIBLE.

□

Henry Busse, NWT Archives

added to that reputation in YK and playing with a Dutch team in The Hague for three seasons. But the hard-driving Byrne, and the North, had made an indelible impression on Shorty Brown. When he came back from Europe, accompanied this time by a Dutch fan who had just become Mrs. Shorty Brown, it was to stay.

Shorty Brown was an outdoorsman by choice, and still is. In his spare time, if he isn't raising money to buy a Zamboni — an ice-making and ice-cleaning machine — for Inuit hockey players in Coppermine, or organizing a Yellowknife team to play in a Hawaiian tournament, you'll probably find him cutting wood at his cabin on the old Discovery Mine site.

Shorty never aspired to be a business magnate. He became one because Norm Byrne discovered that in Shorty Brown he had a guy who'd give his best shot to any job he was handed, whether as a staker, camp boss, equipment operator, prospector, expediter, surveyor, office manager or gofer.

Today, Shorty Brown is in charge of public relations and a vice-president of Bellanca Developments Ltd. Standing on Franklin Avenue and looking south from the heart of Downtown, he can take in no less than four highrise office towers Bellanca has erected, including the New Town's first, the Bellanca Building, in 1972.

Newton Wong and the Pon brothers arrived in

John Poirier,

THE YELLOWKNIFE SKYLINE IN
NOVEMBER, 1989. THREE NEW
TOWERS WERE UNDER
CONSTRUCTION.
☐
THE SKYLINE IN SUMMER, 1989.

Gary Milligan

Henry Busse, NWT Archives

Gary Milligan

Yellowknife seven years after Shorty Brown did, in 1957. Like Wong, whose father had run a laundry in Edmonton since 1912, the Pons had lived in China as youngsters, and knew their father only as an infrequent visitor. It wasn't until Canada's harsh immigration laws were changed in the 1950s that immigrant Chinese men in Canada could send for their families.

The Pons and Wong became friends when they worked in the same Edmonton restaurant. Newton saw an advertisement Jack Glick had placed in an Edmonton paper, offering to lease his Gold Range restaurant, and the three decided to strike out on their own. They barely knew where Yellowknife was.

In 1958 another Edmonton friend, Calvin Mark, joined them. He and Randy Pon did the cooking. Newton and Jimmy were the waiters. The restaurant prospered, and they formed a company — Polar Panda Investments Ltd. — to build a Yellowknife supermarket. YK Foods, a one-storey structure now occupied by the Toronto-Dominion Bank on 49th Street, opened in 1962.

By 1967, when Yellowknife became the Territorial capital, Polar Panda was putting the finishing touches on another project, the Cunningham Building, which would become the Territorial government's first official home when it moved from Ottawa. Yellowknife became a city in 1970.

Marion LaVigne

POLAR PANDA'S FIRST DEVELOPMENT
PROJECT.
(TOP LEFT)
□
YELLOWKNIFE'S MINES HAVE
WORKINGS FAR UNDER THE CITY,
BACK BAY, CENTRE, AND
YELLOWKNIFE BAY, RIGHT.
(LEFT)
□
THE HEART OF DOWNTOWN, 1976.
THE OLD SUPERMARKET, WITH THE
CUNNINGHAM BUILDING, YK'S FIRST
OFFICE TOWER, BEHIND. YK CENTRE
OPENED IN 1972.
(ABOVE)
□
THE CITY'S FIRST SKYWALK.
□
THE COURTHOUSE SERVES ALL THE
WESTERN ARCTIC.

Tessa Macintosh, GNWT

Tessa Macintosh, GNWT

Henry Busse, NWT Archives

Fran Hurcomb

THE PRINCE OF WALES NORTHERN
HERITAGE CENTRE, ON FRAME LAKE.

□

The YK Centre came next, in 1972. YK Foods moved onto its ground floor as the YK Super A food market. Initially four storeys high, the mall was expanded to its present seven storeys in 1973.

Polar Panda added the Court House Building to the Yellowknife skyline in 1978. It opened its Panda I Mall in 1986, and in 1988 added the three-storey Panda II Mall, linked to the YK Mall by the city's first skywalk.

Today, Polar Panda owns some 75,000 square metres of downtown mall and office space and has eighty employees (the Gold Range restaurant was sold to its employees in 1979.) The four partners still take turns restocking shelves, rounding up shopping carts, looking after customers and supervising the staff until the Super A closes each night.

Bellanca Developments and Polar Panda Investments are just two of the companies that have moved the gateway to the North fifteen hundred kilometres, from Edmonton to Yellowknife. They've established the one-time mining town as the commercial and transportation centre of the Western Arctic, as well as the centre of government. And that's given YK a stability few other Northern communities can boast.

Gary Milligan

HENRY BUSSE CLIMBED TO THE ROOF OF THE OLD WILLIAM MCDONALD SCHOOL TO TAKE THIS VIEW OF WHAT IS NOW DOWNTOWN YELLOWKNIFE. BEHIND THE FEDERAL GOVERNMENT APARTMENT BLOCK, THE CAPITAL THEATRE, THE YELLOWKNIFE INN AND THE BAY CAN BE SEEN.
(TOP LEFT)

□

BY 1982, THE COURTHOUSE, THE BELLANCA BUILDING AND THE PRECAMBRIAN BUILDING HAD ALTERED THE SKYLINE CONSIDERABLY.

□

THE SCHOOL WAS DEMOLISHED IN 1982. MILDRED HALL MCMEEKAN'S TINY SCHOOL NOW SITS HERE.

Gary Milligan

Henry Busse, NWT Archives

The Nerco Con and Giant Mines are still major Yellowknife employers, and to this day Yellowknife is the hub of much mining development. That, in turn, has produced strong YK-based aviation and trucking operations. (Mining and tourism fight it out for second spot among Northern employers, behind government.)

Close to a quarter of the NWT's population now calls Yellowknife home — and YK-born Yellowknifers are no longer a novelty. Although "two years and out" was, until the early 1980s, the lifespan of the average southern-born Yellowknifer, long-term Yellowknife residents are no longer as scarce as they used to be.

People in other Northern communities fly their drycleaning to Yellowknife now, not to Edmonton. Many tend to do their shopping in YK too. The recession that chilled southern Canada in the early 1980s passed all but unnoticed in this bustling Northern city.

In 1975, YK had only one convenience store. Today there are corner groceries scattered from one end of the city to the other. There are five shopping malls downtown and a sixth on the drawing boards. There are also booming industrial areas and two major hotels —

IN THE LATE FORTIES INGRAHAM'S NEW HOTEL, LEFT, DOMINATED THE BLOCK WHERE ANDY CLARK'S CENTRE SQUARE AND NORTHERN HEIGHTS BUILDINGS NOW STAND. BEHIND THE HOTEL, THE ORIGINAL FRAME AND PERKINS GARAGE CAN BE SEEN.

□

Gary Milligan

THE CITY CORE FROM THE AIR IN
1989 SHOWS THE NEATLY NUMBERED
STREETS AND AVENUES WHICH
CONTRAST SHARPLY WITH OLD
TOWN'S ANARCHIC LAYOUT.

□

BY 1983, SOME OF THE ORIGINAL
BUILDINGS HAD BEEN INCORPORATED
INTO LARGER ONES, AND MANY HAD
DISAPPEARED COMPLETELY.

□

THE RUTH INCH MEMORIAL POOL
BOASTS A SPECTACULAR VIEW OF
FRAME LAKE, AND A WAVE MACHINE.

Gary Milligan

Ronne Heming

NWT Archives

Gary Milligan

IN BUSSE'S DAY, 54TH STREET
REPRESENTED THE FARTHEST
OUTSKIRTS OF TOWN.
YELLOWKNIFE'S UNITED CHURCH
AND THE YWCA TEAMED UP TO
BUILD NORTHERN UNITED PLACE IN
THE SEVENTIES.

□

both undergoing expansion — plus specialty shops, boutiques and a thriving entertainment sector. A seventeen-storey condominium development on 49th Street near Franklin opened in 1990.

You can buy anything from computers to live Maritime lobsters in Yellowknife's stores. You can shop for Mackenzie Delta parkas or sealskin kamiks from Holman Island, for Inuit sculpture and prints, or for original paintings by local artists whose work is increasingly becoming known Outside.

In the Prince of Wales Northern Heritage Centre, YK boasts a Northern museum that impresses world travellers. Our ultra-modern Stanton Yellowknife Hospital — named after Yellowknife's pioneer doctor — is designed to meet the medical and surgical needs of the Western Arctic, as well as those of Yellowknife itself.

Yellowknife's community arena and curling rink are the envy of many a visitor. And how many southern communities of 15,000 have wave-making equipment in their community swimming pools?

The Ministry of Transport officially opened its new Yellowknife Airport terminal in 1990. The glass-and-chrome palace would jolt oldtimers who remember trying to jam into the cramped little white-painted building erected by Canadian Pacific Airlines, back when the nine-kilometre gravel strip to the airport was the longest road Yellowknife had.

Henry Busse, NWT Archives

Ronne Heming

EXP▶6

EXP▶5

BOMBARDIERS MANOEUVRE ON 51ST
STREET IN THE LATE 1950s. TODAY
THE STREET IS HOME TO
YELLOWKNIFE HARDWARE, STILL
OWNED BY THE ENGLAND FAMILY,
AND A SERIES OF BUILDINGS
CONSTRUCTED BY LONG-TIME
YELLOWKNIFER AND FORMER MINER
ALFREDO AZZOLINI, WHO RAN A
LAUNDROMAT AND SECOND-HAND
STORE IN THE THREE-STOREY
BUILDING RIGHT OF CENTRE.

□

CPA itself is only a memory today, replaced like its lumbering Curtis Commandos and DC-3s by Canadian Airlines International, and by NWT Air, an Air Canada connector. Wide-bodied Boeing 737 jets have cut what used to be an eight-hour milk run to Edmonton to a ninety-five minute direct flight.

There's a new Northern department store on the horizon, to be linked to the Precambrian Building and Bellanca's Northern Centre by skywalks. (The historic Hudson's Bay name, alas, was dropped as part of the deal under which the Bay sold off its Northern stores in 1988.)

Yellowknife no longer exists, as it did in 1934, at the whim of the deputy minister of Northern Affairs (who acted as commissioner of the Northwest Territories as well) and an Ottawa-appointed council. The NWT has had its own full-time commissioner since 1967, and a fully elected legislature since 1983.

Progress has its price, and Yellowknife has paid. Where mosquitoes, break-up, and the price of gold were once YK's main concerns, its worries today are pollution, high taxes, a shortage of housing, environmental protection, interest rates and providing education.

But the real North is still right on our doorstep. It's not unusual, driving home in the dusk of early winter, to see a silver fox ghost across the pavement ahead. Fat, cocky ravens still make life miserable for every dog in town, teaming up to steal food just beyond the maximum length of a chain. In winter, drivers frequently have to brake to avoid the snow-white ptarmigan that congregate within the city limits.

Only a few years ago, a large black bear gave guests in the Explorer Hotel an unexpected thrill when it leaned

John Poirier

Michael Sharpe

YOU CAN STILL FIND PEACEFUL
PLACES ALL AROUND THE BUSTLING
CITY OF YELLOWKNIFE. TOP, BACK
BAY. WILD ROSES GROW IN
PROFUSION, HERE SEEN ON TIN CAN
HILL.

□

up against the floor-to-ceiling windows of the dining room, apparently trying to decide whether to join them. (He debated too long and became dinner, instead; game officers couldn't trap him and haul him back to the bush, so he had to be shot.)

A ten-minute drive will still put you on a lake where you may not see another human being all weekend. The fishing's still good at lakes along the Ingraham Trail, east of Yellowknife, which you can drive to; a half-hour flight in a chartered float plane will land you at a picture-postcard site where an angler's only problem is deciding which of the catch to keep.

Summer or winter, you can watch the float planes or bush planes on skis gliding in to land on Back Bay. And morning or evening, year-round, a mournful chorus of tethered sled dogs still greets the Con Mine's whistle — although most of the huskies are racing dogs, rather than working mutts nowadays.

The gold is still here, too. It's waiting for another Yellowknife Johnnie to start another rush. Or maybe it's just there to daydream about as your campfire's embers die and the molten gold of the Midnight Sun gilds the trees and rock of the Canadian Shield. And, in Old Town, many a sagging cabin still keeps its secrets.

That's Yellowknife: yesterday, today and tomorrow. It's a name to stir the imagination — then and now, and for a long time to come.

Gary Milligan

THE WILDERNESS IS NEVER MORE
THAN TEN MINUTES FROM THE CITY.
☐
NORTHLAND TRAILER COURT,
INSTANT HOUSING FOR THE 90s.
☐
OVER, CONSTRUCTION, 1989.
(JOHN POIRIER)

Walt Humphries